ON THIS BORROWED BIKE

poems

LISA PANEPINTO

THREE ROOMS PRESS

NEW YORK CITY

On This Borrowed Bike

First Edition

ISBN: 978-0-9895125-3-4

Library of Congress Control Number: 2013949710

Cover art:
"Boy Girl" © John Paul (johnpaulpaintings.com)

Cover and interior design:
Kat Georges Design, New York, NY (katgeorges.com)

Text set in Adobe Caslon

Published by Three Rooms Press, New York, NY
threeroomspress.com | facebook.com/threeroomspress

"Every atom belonging to me as good belongs to you"
—Walt Whitman—

"Late at night I get around, pedal 'round this lonesome town on a bicycle"
—Masters of Reality—

"And still this love goes on and on"
—Buffy Sainte-Marie—

CONTENTS

ON THIS
BORROWED BIKE

sounds like midnight

slip into the bed
songs about rising from graves
climb thru windows
black windows where the wind comes thru

the tv by the river pushing down the dam

melted ice fills the streets with dark beer
i glint with the dead drunk trees

she says "you can't hear the song in my head?"
driving in rain night   "it's *unfold*"

it ain't alright by the light of the day
it ain't alright til the night

bringing the bloody silver fish to the river

she shows me the essay
her son wrote   three pages
of handwritten words defending
him leaving an animal to waste

i shot that moose
and let it get old
my uncles were up to the point drinking
i didn't have anyone to help carry it out
that moose got old

sparks

new needle on the turntable
makes the music go thru
me like a meteor shower

so loud it breaks me
into starry pieces   makes me
shower light

the sky moving
a soft pink lip

fire to the edge of sight

gin june

i met my baby
at the baby bar in red light

we played the jukebox
in psychic rhythm

him asking what song
i wanted
flipping thru the discs

me saying #s only
but reading the poetics

my heart a thunder
bb king

so glad people
don't have to carry me thru
esther phillips

i know my maker lives
because he lives inside me

records from the land
of believing we are god

high eyed   wet
thru the trees

i just drank anything
handed to me

crow chase day

flooded fields and berries
dripping down
to kiss the water

sneak a moment of sun
in the straw
bossman would want me behind
the computer still
breaking my hands   not hearing
the joyous singing
from somewhere across
the river   a kid counting off random
numbers to the bog water & dead
trees as family smiles
at him   a girl's voice answering
from the bog   dog bark
frog jumping out of the moss

like stories   my hands   like mud
where trees grow
what's going on crow?
you go thru the leaves
of the trees   thru rain
thru rooftops   black god
breath of rain

times when you leave

i become blue as the spring
longing to be in that valley
where you walk   a flush of burgundy
longing to bring my love to the sea

i crawl under the willow
& turn to small pieces of bone
apple blossom   rain filled
seed   use my head as soil

the sky whispers me back alive
covers me in wild flowers
roots around my limbs
wind thru my ribs

i pick the red buds from the gutter
make a robe to wear
i pick the wet white petals of fruit trees
fill my mouth with song

wild turkeys

this morning you wanted
to disappear

then wind came through
leaves saying you are
wrapped in cedar
forest song
violet flower

three wild turkeys in cloud
eat bees
wait to rise in the breeze

unsnag your lungs
they say
come with us

back to me

come back to the pacific   with only one shirt   finding it strange
the rails full of trains   highways of trucks   god cage churches
soot sky   river ash   that keeps moving   soft and swift   no
matter what is done to it

return to the fields along the highway   where snow falls on
hundreds of canadian geese   fly over the settlement   to the
temple   at the breast of a hill   where i am going to commit
myself   as i would an asylum   to forest paths   where i feel i
can run forever   light over fresh powder   to the rushing lurch of
the orange burlington northern   with its steel feet and heavy
boxcars   making the earth surrender   to my running body
relaxing into infinity   and opening wide to encompass the bodies
of all human animals

return to the red pine   to black dam and vodka blue waters   to
hills of wheat   covered in frost   to embody you

come back clicking your tongue to the blues   smelling like tobacco
to the basement of the flour mill   where old chinese artists serve
green tea   and ease human suffering   to watch how ducks
searching for food in frozen pond are more alive than anything
to the steamy greenhouse   to the fountain   to soothe me with
water sounds and make me high with wishing coins

come back to the river   that keeps moving   soft and swift   no
matter what is done to it

crow q & a

1   fog rolled in river

where are you going?

from the heart of the tree
to the belly of the tree

    to dance

with the potion moon
with the ribbon sun

how do you know?

dawn comes with our call
night comes with caress

our veins map the wind
our mouths full of sky

a web of kin brings our song
from storm to calm

what do you see?

when everything
is coming and going

sound shape cloud skin
coyote feast lynx light

what do you smell?

balsam pollen bone
blood musk rain

what do you say?

humans black cloud
hawk owl
worms lodging
dead fox
we praise the day

2   branch magic pick me up

you're always there beside me?

we carry your wishes and bloom from your shadow
a flash of grace

you'll never drown   we'll caw you back and lift you

what songs do you know?

we're still here the first and last

to give back the roots
to give back the rocks
to put back the dusk
to know where you're at

we'll turn to other galaxies

do you ever feel like a motherless child?

she's the silent glide   daring eggs fog lung

would you sing to me all day?

when you can't hear my three beats   i'm still singing behind
your eyes

what's it like behind my eyes?

tender blue   don't be afraid to swim

was it you who brought the field of wild pansies to the lawn?

because you left those peanuts in the snow
we also planted queen anne's lace   daisy   maple seed

did you leave your feather in the trail for me?

to guide your love

3   infinite flight

what's your favorite tree?

pine   the best vantage for touching sky

how do you fly the winter?

burn with the heat of branches
light a highway remembering

you stay protected   you stay immune?

we hear the gun come out before it sparks

you cross the river and back again?

break from eternity   death brings flowers

are all gods black?

black is universe
black is trust

where do you come from?

clam digging by the rocky shore in rain
the seams of life
woods and moss and tide

crow jane

spider webs on the bridge
cast out deals with the wind
sail me some food   i'll weave you some luck

dirty loads   a thousand trucks
cut me up like chicory   lily   rose
bottles tossed on dead leaves

try to hold my head so high
like crow jane   her witchy walk's
the only thing i like about this scene

snake skin & umbrella cane
pipe tobacco rubbed in stone
tide pools of sweat and bone

they bring their boats thru anyway
yellow fish   broken wish

come in threes

you said "everyone passed is inside me"
as i counted time
by the programs on public radio
the hours moving fast in your arms
bbc coming on
the tarot card i drew
III
someone standing
on a ridge
looking at the sea   with back turned
a new journey   in between
3 wand trees
your skin sounded like seashells

*

we both dreamt of floods
now the blues on the radio
interrupted for flood warnings
the river swelling
the blues back on
the rain heavy
i stare into the wet pines so hard
i become them
i want to become you   at least for a little while

*

feather hair
brown rice skin
feeling the brush
of your fingers
over me
ghost blessings
my limbs welled with water
& memory float

river crackling
ice coming in   talking
in communion

we're going to protect
this soft river underbelly
we're going to be a shield of living
freeze in yellow air

being born is so holy   so easy
i summon you here
with these words   i summon you to my lips

on this borrowed bike

we found leaning
in the night against
the old shed where
the white cat jumped
from   on this bike
that belonged to the dead
that belonged to the
teenager made dead
in a car crash
on this bike
i can go through
boulders i can move
through cars i can go
through people's bodies
i can go through
trees i can fly without
looking i can fly
steadily without looking
lifting like a crow
without anyone
on this bike i can
rise above ditches
bounce up from potholes
ride over thick
grass into river
where light bounces
white silver in the
lick of waves
mesmerizes me so
i cannot read
just cling to the bench
on the dock
a quiet guardian
glancing at the loving
going on to my right

at the fishing
going on to my left
the changing leaves
leaping softly
with the bike of the dead
lent to me by her father
the bike that lets
me go through
these things untouched
rusted bare bone
handlebar tied
with sweetgrass
but otherwise ok
we got after i sat melting
in the parking lot
of grocery store sipping
on bike water bottle
full of rolling rock
that drowsed me numb
with motionless
bottled star light
that when we pulled
up outside your house
i said got any
porpoise left
you said yes a ton
and brought back
the butter container full
of chunks
of porpoise
taken from the bay
with a spear
i glanced at the darkness
of it and closed
the container   ashamed

at taking the holy
animal meat
and when you dropped
me off i savored
its thick richness
in the dark stairwell
then climbed the stairs
and fell heavily
to sleep with the ocean
and the animal
and the spear and your
seasonings   your onions
and peppers in my belly

and dreamt of taking
care of babies after
seeing the old dying
dog limp out
to the yard

on this bike
i ride into
the bog off the edge
of the trail where the bare
dead trees expose the pond
i ride in
without a crash
just a soft
circle in the water
like the beavers
make and when
i come out
i have the thoughts
of beaver
the thoughts
of porpoise

and they have my thoughts

the smell of wet rot ground of dying flowers fallen leaves in the wet canopy air green and gray above mud so black and rich you could live off it

driving

japan got bombed   the dust in the ocean   even the fisherman's
tuna made people sick   you were a driver in georgia working on a
movie set   at the gas pump someone jeered   i wouldn't do your
job for a million bucks   pointing at the black kids in the backseat
they're just kids you said

there were always horses coming   the songs on the radio
orchestrating peace & forgiveness   you were old as the war   & i
was young as the sun   i would ride where the feet should be and
feel the road right under me   a fish flapped from the bottom of a
lincoln   dead raccoon laid in the dust   blue jay flash &
present wings eating round the magic tree   in the house of the
rising sun   all the life and people roaming

night stream

last night walking   the sobbing of a woman   primal screams of
someone   breaking   we went side by side into the dark woods
with the banging & dogs barking & a woman wailing   til the
police came   a crown of blood is a lick of rain   blends fast with
animal tracks   we are not dead we are dreaming   we breathe in
the trees   fox lay sleeping   pine dogs wake   how might we love
each other?   by lying next to each other in soft fur

at the folk festival

we saw a shadow kid on the green bridge night   who didn't look
up from his texting   we seemed to walk thru   made me think of
jl   indian kid who jumped off that bridge   after being chased and
harassed by the cops   still haven't found her body   across the
river   prayer singer backed by drummers sang holy   bald eagle
came up low to listen   then flew under the green bridge   cast
blue around my grateful heart   the farmer poets said they learn
rhythm by the rhythm of the land & the milking of the cows
always sing as you work   a lady with child voice in old body sang
about orange stars & sweet milk   gold eye glitter   dancey river
matchbox may baskets   from the beer tent   my friend said   this
girl can go anywhere   & we rode our bikes home in hurricane
night

mediation

i'm a cloud of grief you said   an open wound   i said no you're a
wing of breeze   then sought counsel with the living trees   oldest
being   color of stone & birch   river maker picked me up and
made me   i saw crisp silver   a thousand fish eye rush   a
thousand wings went by   turned me to cool pebbles   brushed by
fish petals   lungs shook loose and flew   take all of me i can't go
back   cause river sees all of me   lifts my light   drinks the
rapids   salmon flight   gives a push & rides on   brown wings
big as god   and my ribs and my lips   heave thank you   got
past drowning   three eagles whispered god

harvest party

we walk in and see   stodge professors in vests drinking wine
my friend greets us   whispers   a lot of anti-landfill crowd here
the out of state syringes leak down river to indian island   i
migrate to the fire   tales begin   the hunt for a leaning cedar to
get dry wood   its flames of yellow sun   lady of the swamp
makes you cold with cruel thoughts   spirits run round the houses
kids' voices playing in the moon   don't open the door   you'll be
fine   a moth coat in the closet   that dust leather had a back of
wings   all furry   one came down from the light   made us go
silent   then wandered up again   there's always been a ghost in
the house   but it's not evil or the dogs would bark

down in pawn

the cat brought back a bird each morning   the winter you
threatened to go away   when you see me with long beard & rags
living downtown don't come near   you pawned the gun
clarinet   metronome   lost time   where you used to be

eternal

ghost reflection   eternal white birch   crow caw   eternal chrome
ice black eye   eternal glacier melt   motor stream   eternal heart
rush   mother hands   eternal invisible shelter   eternal river
entrance   eternal river exit   eternal rock embrace   eternal
becoming something true   eternal mind scream   cedar birth   red
buds   eternal child song   steam plant hammer   eternal lost me
i am right here   eternal don't leave me   i am right here   eternal
island sail   rib wail   eternal silver sight   eternal lost someone
canadian flight   eternal arrest this man   he shot my brother
eternal black god   eternal flood bank   leaf food   eternal siren
call   eternal rescue all   eternal sorry mood   clean streets   silent
body   eternal pulse song   eternal hi ice where you been   i am
right here   eternal i am becoming someone new   eternal trust

across the river

on the edge and in need of love
wet cold keeps us together

songs along the bank
giving the shore legs

drowned boys run by
their feet falling

silently on pine needles
the trees greet their sons

not much

hungry
i eat the sun & rain

squirrels
approach me

tell me where to find
their hidden caches

for the loins of the night
i hallucinate

enough

she tells me she'll be
getting some money
from the canadian government
got a payment
a few years back
because they sprayed
agent orange on her tribal
lands   now it's proven they sprayed
agent purple
and agent white too

she played in those woods as a kid
waded thru   swam in it
the orange pine was sick
and spreading   the smell of wet
earth was cursed

my dad died young
my mom died young
my brother fell down
when i visited him   agents poisoned

the thunder   a shock of moan
lightning walks with blinded
eyes of a vanished
animal   turns to deafening shriek

she's had headaches since she was a kid
walks with tumors in her feet
what have they done
to the most holy ones?
what money is
enough?

waiting room

crunch of fan motor   acid drag
of vehicles outside
mixed with crickets & wind
news on the tv
the tide's on fire

the mechanic said
your car can't breathe
& is leaking oil
as good as dead

they wash the pelicans
they poison
on petroleum soil

sound of people moving
who i don't know

how could i be left here
a broken mirage
& no place to go

one of our houses

sound of water
everywhere
one of our houses
has burned

smoke on everything
ghostly opaque
on pictures of women
going into fields
black and the windows
blown out
on cemetery
& peony

handing burnt remnants
out the window
into rain
my face charred
my legs raw

wild distance

to think my soul is
big enough to stretch
across the continent

a wing on each shore

and god is a deer
with fresh antlers
at the top of
golden butte
looking at me

for ryan

you said you'd be my
metaphysician   and that the light
from car headlights on dark
ceiling was really the shine
of us passing
thru dimensions

bird sparks
as i rushed
riding bike from work
thru parking lot made me
stop & smile thanks to god

the book at your kitchen
table spoke of dolphin
intelligence as universal pulse

you sang to me
about getting lost
& how each night you
dream of being a soldier

for lucy

days when i wear
your crucifix
around and pray to paper

dreamt of you
giving me
packages of incense

flock of birds flying
fast erratic joyous
thru snow flurry sky

sound of my heart

for elmore

go ahead and say
how the forest was
a spread of lung
spilling vapor & smiling

don't be disheartened
the world needs poets
just as much
as it needs farmers

say it over and over
how the pine needles smell
after the rain   the fallen
trees so blue   the wind
so strong   i wanted
to go with it

spokane

in night streets a car rode behind us slow
a girl rolled down the window   yelled meth meth meth
we caught up to them at stop sign
they were young blonde sunken cheeks laughing
want some meth? we shook our heads no   they drove

back here with its curse   all of us
either in it or recovering
river poisoned so the whole town poisoned
d talked about the shotgun pulled on us
partying in crack house sleeping on pool table
thinned out   hallucinating in back seats
driven thru drunk streets   dark forests
not caring if we stepped into the other side
surviving on halos
j tried to kill himself
& here me loved by the clouds
don't let the gray suck him down
let water be his god always

*

butte top
wind pines
wind speaking
you kissed me and light shined
you were me   i was you

we meet at night by the stone in the woods and be washed

*

sparrow flew to me in airport
it was looking for me   it was god

my heart was saying please
don't die   stay with me   music
will teach us how to fly

on a plane thru a layer of pink sunrise

my water filled body

wake in parking lot
in fog realizing
you're in a separate vessel
your chariot
wake before dawn
in warm fur
crickets out

a ghost hugged me
her eyes shining oceans
a ghost blessed me

the car engines
lulled me night
long

thru redneck bangs
& singing
predawn

i'm a good old boy
my mama loves me

diesel rig sounds wrapped
me safely in sleep

going to the town
of bath
to get cleansed

tree stumps with bouquets
of flowers

giant gods have taken
my hands & are leading
me on now
and the wind has become so
soft and leading

spread me out
into everything

people painting all
over the sea

people finding me
so lightly bathed
in bone & rush eyed

i know
finding this ocean
is it

limping seagulls
and god sun

i'm just a sprawl of earth
and other people
my cotton clothes from field
my water filled body
panting on grasses
growing from live sand
painted blood like trees
and seagull mouths

the holy sky grows me
and the shine
waves play with boats
play people
play rocks

the sand talks
turning to glass
the waves talk back yes

thank you to whoever
made my night kind
made my life so clean
& clear & full of music
& wind
i can run again

happy woman blues

you know
i'm a happy woman
i wouldn't try to take
my life

we find her
coming back from the bar
in gold bridge light

she's in her underwear
begging for a cigarette laughing
hoarsely   we tell her how search
and rescue is looking
for her in lit up
boats   as drunks
discuss her death

we drive her home and find
she's destroyed
everything   not one thing
went untouched
she laughs   glass
covers the floor
with pages of books
crushed baskets   food
dumped from the fridge
let's do a pill

we put her to bed
her lover just out of prison
shelving ripped books
without shirt or shoes
he steps on the glass   tells

me my voice goes
straight to his soul   gives
me his number

i have not had enough to drink
and must wake up
for work in the morning
to care for flowers and shrubs
in vast mansion gardens

blues authority

sleeping in the backseat
of my car
just off main street
behind the bar
i woke to a crying man
and a woman screaming
at him "there's blood all over"
and him saying "you
don't care about me"

how i would have
liked to take him
in the backseat with me
and clean his wounds
and love him but stayed
concealed in dark
blankets
the sun rising directly
into my car

blues from the vfw

an eddy came from the bottom of the lake
a cold gust wherever i went

i dug a pit each place i stood
roots emerged from seeds the dead left

doctor dan was hank williams under his stetson
the scar shone thru his eyes
shrieking out the blues
playing on the pinewood floor
his ashes made a haul of bone

the names of the dead were written on the ceiling
we were all beneath the grave

guts spilled on the floor
they became smoke at my feet
they became a woman and man dancing
my mother and father
entangled by a crazed and lonesome chord
winking at me with eye and teeth

they moved the waves so gracefully
rolled their hips and birthed the wind
they didn't know we were inside
a dive of battered soldiers

on the floor alone
fragile and holy and lighting us
i rocked   i nodded   i knew them
there was nothing to say

their shoulders shook and freed the dead
doctor dan threw back his head
laughed at beauty heat come out of bone

when the band was done me and the dead
staggered up the stairs
dancing from the sand   out to the red pine
to be born from swamp bottom

unfortune

he shot the young bear come visit
said he'd never seen a bear not scared

come right up to the porch
could have got the dog

the bear had human hands
when he dragged it to the road

god son
flesh moon

under the night
we hung our heads

private property

become greener
than green leaf
raven wood

an ash hush

trudging white

snap sticks
slide on licks of
mud   marvel at naked
birch   paint them blue
so you don't   get lost

plow thru
bones & dirt

roof shingle heaps
& budweiser cans

as penance for
becoming numb

let the new ferns
take your lungs

lying on the hotel bed   he says to me

my plants

thrive at sixty degrees

i will set the temperature low

for my plants

and die around them

and they will grow all

around me   agave flower from

my heart   mountain laurel from

my mouth   and you will die

and be lain on the ground

and the crows

will carry you away

and i will eat

the crows

visiting you in the afterlife

the door is open to the rain
in a house of antiques

you have become
good at playing guitar
from a cedar tree

talking about riding
your motorcycle
in the north
standing on ridges
looking out
at the sea
swimming a lot
clearing out buildings
to hang art

you're wearing
your cowboy hat
and grinning

i offer to get you high
but you don't
need it anymore

in the mountains
you are singing

river metallic as veins of saints

the land creates
its inhabitants

here i am low
down   bog like

making myself remember

motion is medicine

on the road alone

thinking of the one
who gave me

a room full of color
to get well in

half in the earth
of river island   children

beating life upstairs
a bed on the floor

to dream like the spirits dream

*

in quebec i can walk forever
and live on ale   coffee   cigarettes

my memories return
and relive themselves

on these streets

hard to sleep
in a room full of strangers   but i pretend
they are angels   here to protect me

the sunset a pink bloom
from ground
to sky   opening itself
from dusk
like the arms of a saint

every moment is deja vu

shadows of ghosts
pull out chairs
open doors for me

prisons turned to art
museums

painted tulips
our resurrection

picasso's on slabs of oak

i have visions of where
the trees were cut
from

and crawl within
the color

triangle head

square legs

sea urchin breasts

reenter the world

in picasso shape

*

marinara sauce tastes like tears

french speaking youth
bum american cigarettes
saying   cool   after my responses

and a jazz singer on the stereo
let me fly away

teeth grinder

i know when
my skull surges
thru open sky at dawn

leaving trails of bone dust
electric tongue
finely tuned

wind rushes me
glitters me over the bridge
a moon in my mouth

birds pull
my sharpened
stars

beneath the waves

a friend calls crying in the morning
her indian teen cousin jumped
off the tallest bridge in town   haven't found
her body in the river cops chased her
watched her jump come up for air then not come up

it's not on the news that she's lost to the river
a fly nearly invisible floating thru
the room like dust white kid jumps from tallest bridge and they search
for days reporters are everywhere but indian kid jumps
and they say current's too strong don't search at all
no body found   spirit loose alone
breaks the skin   floods us thru

say a prayer for that kid now
there was nothing wrong with you

river love that kid now
take that kid home
have a bed in rain for that kid to sleep in

soft river bank single lost goose
purse dropped butterfly flip over the tallest bridge

the laughing wind   say she is a river god now
the pink sea gold rising from the waves

guantanamo

american flags from red wounds
blue bruises   shredded pulp
of human flesh
people torn from ancestral lands
for brown skin   blankets
of blood   bouquets
of ripped muscle
stomped light
crushed back   broken bones
blown up
balloon hands
heads drowned   chained to cold
concrete   starved & suffocated   forced
to take drugs   american citizens safe
comfortable   from the agony
& murder
of brown people

the night becomes strange

1   she has been sick in bed all day

i climb in with her and her five-year-old son   happy
as she smiles and touches me lightly
i tell her my hidden dreams   she spits
silver from her mouth
i catch it with mine and it turns
to beer   i become
loose-fleshed and gray and sink
into the basement   my mouth
darker & more full of beer   i watch the quick
and the dead and wake
running through streets of ice
and slush   to airport runways
that end at the surf
where grasses are
stiff brown & pressed by clouds of light

2   night and i stare out the window

of johnny's restaurant   my reflection
in the dark glass coming
over the dam   i cannot bear to look
at and eat my fish & chips   i ride
my bike from bar to bar along route 2 and see
my name on tv screens as i play electronic trivia
games   i am winning   someone at the end of the bar
says   congratulations amy! "who's amy?" i look over
to confirm it's me and he says "that's perfect"

the man next to me says "thought you'd be
out with your boyfriend?" i say "no letting my youth
go to waste" and ride

3   at woodman's grill men are talking about fishery

and the snake river dams   "don't talk about me
that way" i say   as emaciated
musicians look straight ahead and bang
their heads against loose gray   and young
hippies dance with long blondes   i lay on
the ice by some trailer and dream of staying
that way forever   but zip my coat and get back on
my bike that brings me over slick hills and honking
trucks   to the porch steps of my home   where
a giant is smoking   whose waist i hug
and say   "i don't feel very happy"

4   there's a party across the street

i smell grief
in wet rotted wood   from the gray
shed door warm fog
night i smoke
a santa fe cigarillo
the first drag good and the rest nasty   i toss the heavy
stick to brown ice & smoke
my mind   she is folding
laundry inside   i say i whistled
but you didn't
hear   she says
you started smoking
again i say no   she comes to
tell me i overload
the washing machine   the beach
come to visit me in city
streets   sits on my bed
under christmas lights   saying
the music reminds her of irish people killing

each other   people at war
wearing burlap clothing

5   at the edge of my bed for hours   her eyes

are black bodied
and strong   it feels like a vision
the type where homeless
drunks discover god   it makes me laugh
and cry   hollow and broken   then warm
and healed

when she leaves   i listen
to the radio   wanting
to both hide under the covers forever   and go
running to meet
the dawn

black wet
asphalt in the snow in the shape
of a heart
builds my life
from snow

6   the air off my icy river is fresh

and washes the blues
from my biking self   the streets are sun colored sand water
that turn my face and clothes to mud   pebbles
lodged in my eyes and between my teeth   i am metallic
bronze and made of street dirt   smelling of street
rain   the sound of my voice is gritty and my eyes cracked
rocks   my bike is an excavated relic taken
from the earth   formerly ridden by river ghosts   coming home

in a night storm   snowflakes turn to feathers
that pillow the asphalt   as the river nods
at the glory of my bridge crossing   my bare racing
tires sled the soft white streets   sheets i lay down in
and listen to the radio from   strange when the radio is all
static   i hear the voice of a 2-year-old boy say
someone's name over and over   into the suck of dark
basement   i hear the laughter of 13-year-old girls   and how
the moon is bothered by the crunch
of dirty snow under foot   i hear a voice in the kitchen
whisper to me about cancer and vomiting blood   i hear my brother
calling from the other side of the world   and the first thing
he says is "how
do you spell 'tomorrow'?"

i open your coat

to the smell of damp earth roots
bark leaves
cedar   pine   blossoming

smell of clouds   the mud
standing softly
on your boots   closing my eyes

some of the world's poetics
bend into me   some of the ocean
enters my eyes

and i bring my river
into you   bluely

farewell ride

going to new brunswick where the tides are most
extreme on earth

paula's in the driver seat   maggie's sitting shotgun
the three of us coast
along curves of faded white lines down skinny back roads

carried away by the pull   drinking breeze
hash smoke   laughing in big black
cadillac thru sparkling

farmland in fall atlantic foliage   big red apples
grow at the sides of the road
waiting for juicy mouths

going to a place where the sun is sailing and the river comes in
brown and alive after returning to mud
so quick it will take you

going to a great northern peak where everything you do and say
and feel is a peak
where mountains lip the sea

stopping on a hillside of indian graves
beside small ancient chapel above the water
where paula & maggie's mother lies buried

listening to wish you were here
god waiting there with us   high and amazed

a day where i feel my father joined to me
by wrist and heart sitting in the backseat

and we get out to sit on their mother's grave

the dead turned to cosmos   goldenrod
new red and yellow buds watering me

prayerful on the grass
nothing but love
for the women and high land

the idea of moving away
returned to the tide

getting on the bus

the wind lifts
the dumpster lid
and the water crashes
over the dam
the wind lifts
my hood   & turns my down
jacket into puffy
wing feathers

i laugh and rise
into the silver clouds
and know what it is
for god to take you
to die and go
with the spirits
to be in flight

*

i see you in my yard
and feel lucky
you're visiting me
sad i'm not home for it
am just rising
then remember

i will have to
come back down

*

i get on the bus
and go to work

a black haired girl gets on
the bus and closes her
eyes in prayer

a blond girl prays
to music like me

the girls put
their legs together
in stranger-intimacy loving each
other in passing light

*

comes the low sudden
choir of kids
husking an ocean hymn

me wanting to be no one
picked up by the wet tongues
outside and taken away

*

a knocked down
sun floating on the flood
my fingers wet with rain
red paint seeping
from bus stop telephone poles
neko case thru headphones

a hawk flies past
looking into me
then rising
directly over my head

*

i would love all the lonely
kids on the bus
i would make them feel ok

i pray with all the people
on the bus
we all open our wet hands
smooth and growing blooms
and we pray

we make new scenes out
the window
we weep in extreme
sorrow & joy

our landscapes blend

we visit the water in each other's bodies
the sound of waves in lungs

curled in gold   tide light
bloom of shore   silver breasted sky

gust licks our bedding   penetrates
our dreams leaves skin on our waking

musk leans our pines   black eyed
in silver waves

the vulnerability of being
birds at sea in rain

blue dream

i strummed a sad song   a & c
in the dark rain   thinking
of passing from this
world   talking about chi   not the wave
but in the wave

leaves in death

skin like petals   apples

walk singing a star
fish song on
the bottom of the sea

you say i want to record that

we drink each other
in the kitchen   now play
the gold guitar   rain
on tin

white seed fields   take pictures

the kitchen light flickin on
saying hi to visitors

waves turn
to songs

Acknowledgments

Thank you water, sun, wind, trees, Annie Finch, Joy Harjo, Debra Marquart, Patricia Smith, Peter Carlaftes, Kat Georges, Three Rooms Press, Michael T. Fournier, Rebecca Griffin, Cabildo Press, Esther Attean, Marlene Charron, my friends, family, teachers, birds, spiders, music, stars, and my love, Ryan Roderick, thank you for all your magic, light and sustenance.

About the Author

Lisa Panepinto is a poet, writer, radio host and performer. She is the author of the chapbook *Island Dreams* and poetry editor for *Cabildo Quarterly*. Her writing has appeared in the *Accompanist, Maine Peace Action Committee, River Pine Anthology of Civic Discourse*, and *Maintenant*. She holds degrees from Washington State University and the University of Southern Maine, and currently lives in Pittsburgh.

Books on Three Rooms Press

PHOTOGRAPHY-MEMOIR

Mike Watt
On & Off Bass

FICTION

Michael T. Fournier
Hidden Wheel

Janet Hamill
Tales from the Eternal Café

Eamon Loingsigh
Light of the Diddicoy

Richard Vetere
The Writers Afterlife

DADA

*Maintenant: Journal of
Contemporary Dada Art & Literature
(Annual poetry/art journal, since 2003)*

SHORT STORY ANTHOLOGY

*Have a NYC: New York Short Stories
Annual Short Fiction Anthology*

HUMOR

Peter Carlaftes
A Year on Facebook

PLAYS

Madeline Artenberg &
Karen Hildebrand
The Old In-and-Out

Peter Carlaftes
*Triumph For Rent (3 Plays)
Teatrophy (3 More Plays)*

Larry Myers
*Mary Anderson's Encore
Twitter Theater*

TRANSLATIONS

Patrizia Gattaceca
Isula d'Anima / Soul Island
(poems in Corsican with
English translations)

George Wallace
EOS: Abductor of Men
(American poems with Greek translations)

POETRY COLLECTIONS

Hala Alyan
Atrium*

Peter Carlaftes
*DrunkYard Dog
I Fold with the Hand I Was Dealt*

Joie Cook
When Night Salutes the Dawn

Thomas Fucaloro
*Inheriting Craziness is Like
  a Soft Halo of Light
It starts from the belly and blooms*

Patrizia Gattaceca
Isula d'Anima / Soul Island

Kat Georges
*Our Lady of the Hunger
Punk Rock Journal*

Robert Gibbons
Close to the Tree

Karen Hildebrand
*One Foot Out the Door
Take a Shot at Love*

Matthew Hupert
Ism is a Retrovirus

David Lawton
Sharp Blue Stream

Jane LeCroy
Signature Play

Dominique Lowell
*Sit Yr Ass Down or You Ain't gettin
  no Burger King*

Jane Ormerod
*Recreational Vehicles on Fire
Welcome to the Museum of Cattle*

Lisa Panepinto
On This Borrowed Bike

Angelo Verga
Praise for What Remains

George Wallace
*Poppin' Johnny
EOS: Abductor of Men*

Three Rooms Press | New York, NY

Current Catalog: www.threeroomspress.com
Three Rooms Press Is Distributed by PGW

CPSIA information can be obtained at www.ICGtesting.com
Printed in the USA
LVOW13s1141240114

370832LV00005B/11/P